FAREWELL to Old England

New York in Revolution

D0840463

by Ellen F. Rosebrock

South Street Seaport Museum
16 Fulton Street, New York

Library of Congress Cataloging in Publication Data
Rosebrock, Ellen Fletcher.
    Farewell to Old England.
    Bibliography: p.
    1. Rose, Joseph. 2. Sears, Isaac, ca. 1730–1786. 3. Low, Isaac,
1735–1791. 4. New York (City) — Commerce — History. 5. New York (City) —
History — Colonial period, ca. 1600–1775. I. Title.
HC102.5.A2R675   330.9'747'103   75–3941
ISBN 0–913344–21–4

Produced by the Publishing Center for Cultural Resources, New York City
Design: Janet Czarnetzki
Manufactured in the United States of America

Research and publication made possible by a grant from the National Endowment for the
Humanities. Related display, "Farewell to Old England," which opened at the South Street
Seaport Museum in May 1976, made possible in part by grants from the National Endow-
ment for the Humanities and the New York State Council on the Arts.

Acknowledgments

Farewell to Old England could hardly have become a manuscript, let
alone a small book with pictures in it, without the valuable help of
a great many people. To Mary Black, Curator of Paintings, Sculpture
and Decorative Arts at the New-York Historical Society; and to Floyd
M. Shumway author of *Seaport City,* I am especially grateful, for it was
their thoughtful reading and their comments on the text at an early
stage that added in many ways to its quality. Peter Stanford and Philip
Yenawine, too, contributed important early evaluations. To the en-
thusiastic researches of Joanna B. Dean, Dorian Harris and Mark
Lovewell I owe the sparkle of several illustrations and some piquant
details. Jan Hudgens of the New-York Historical Society's print room
spent many a cheerful hour showing piles of pictures to avid lookers, as
did Charlotte La Rue of the Museum of the City of New York, and the
staff of the print department at the New York Public Library. Terry
Walton's serendipitous discovery of Joseph Rose's small white grave-
stone literally at the eleventh hour made that wonderful man a little
more real to everyone who thinks about Rose's life in revolutionary
New York. And to Mike Gladstone, Frank Dobo and Janet Czarnetzki
of the Publishing Center for Cultural Resources goes the credit for
turning the manuscript into a small book.

Ellen F. Rosebrock

Preface

The World Turned Upside Down" was the tune the brass band played as the British army surrendered to the American upstarts and their French allies at Yorktown, but *Farewell to Old England* shows that for some New Yorkers at least, the world carried on through and after the Revolution in much the same way as it always had.

What follows is an engrossing account of the careers of three New York merchants who lived through the years of rebellion. These were the men who, with scores of others like them, laid the city's commercial foundations well. From those foundations the next generation quickly built their city into the new republic's leading port. In *Farewell to Old England* we meet Joseph Rose, first a mariner, later a shipmaster and merchant. He lived in New York during the turbulent pre-war years, lived in his city during the occupation, and stayed on there after the peace. The story follows, too, Rose's townsmen and contemporaries: the radical privateer Isaac Sears and the rich, aristocratic merchant Isaac Low.

Through the story we can see that although the New York of two hundred years ago was a more perilous — perhaps even a more exciting — place than it is today, the motives, dreams and desires of its people then were scarcely different from our own. Any reader will surely come away from this account with a greater understanding of the New Yorkers who lived through the years of the Revolution — especially of those who chose, for reasons powerful to them, to remain in the city under British occupation.

Altogether, this account works like a puzzle in which the intimate stories of three waterfront merchants and their families provide perfectly fitting pieces that complete a portrait of the city in a complex and disrupted period of its long history.

Mary Black

*Old and solid and wise in 1799, these three men —
like the men met in the narrative that follows — lived
through the Revolution. One can only guess what
happened to them in the decades that followed 1763,
what choices they made between liberty and loyalty;
but in the last days of the 18th century these men
who were adults in the years of revolution were
joined by a younger generation to bring New York to
the preeminence in waterborne trade that fulfilled the
promise inherent in the city since its founding
(courtesy of the New-York Historical Society).*

Table of Contents

Joseph Rose, sea captain, merchant and New Yorker, was born in 1735. The years of the Revolution occupied most of his adult life; he died at 72 in 1807. The time-smoothed stone that marks his grave stands in Trinity's north churchyard, and on it, nearly effaced, this legend is carved: "His children and the poor are left/ to lament a faithful father." Next to him lies Barbara his wife, and close to Barbara is their grandchild Mary Adeline (photograph by Edmund V. Gillon Jr.).

Introduction

Fizz, boom and dazzle and the silver burst of bottle rockets over quiet bays for two proud centuries: Liberty and the Fourth of July! Independence Hall and Boston Town Meeting! Like a tricolored screen the symbols of an American iconography cover the long ago realities of doubt, hesitation, fear — and loyalty.

We'd all confidently be patriots now, seeing history with the privileged vision of hindsight. But to men living then, decades of real life had to be lived around the great emergencies of revolution, and there were awesome decisions that each man had to make.

Loyalty to England was bred into Americans with their religion; and like the powerful God of the Old Testament, the King was invincible. That he might act unwisely was admitted, and when he began to effect measures that threatened American commerce, the spirited protest came from all ranks. But protest was not revolution, and the range of political opinion between the two poles was wide. Nowhere were so many different points of view held by the members of a single population as in New York, and this diversity characteristic of our city throughout its history earned it a reputation for political instability, in those 13 pre-revolutionary years.

Farewell to Old England centers on a man named Joseph Rose, typical of thousands of men whose names are forgotten today. He built a house on Water Street near Peck Slip three years before the fight for independence began. And vastly strengthening the reality that man has for us who think of him today is the presence of his 1807 tombstone of carved and weathered marble in the north graveyard of ancient Trinity Episcopal Church. Rose was a sea captain and a small merchant, and he appears to have been more interested in the details of his life and work than he was in politics. His decisions during the 20 years of trouble amounted to loyalty (he stayed on at his house in British-occupied New York), but at the end of the war he chose America over loyalist emigration. Two other men are considered as well: both were Episcopalians with Rose, but they represent political positions closer than Rose's to each extreme. Isaac Low, a courtly man of family and fortune, was dedicated to reconciliation with England: in addition to his moral commitment to the Crown, he valued England's protection and patronage of colonial commerce. When revolution became inevitable, Low had no choice but loyalty. Isaac Sears, the fiery Sons of Liberty's lieutenant, was a born radical; and as Joseph Rose loved normality Sears thrived on the excitement of rebellion.

Throughout the 20 years of trouble, a powerful instinct to "get on with the work" influenced the actions of men in commerce in New York. They wanted to make fortunes more than they wanted to make news, and most were anxious to find workable solutions to their problems safely within the old relationship with England. Commerce to them was part of the Lord's work. It was the virtuous industry that built cities.

This diligent preoccupation with work drew some men back to the city as loyalists under the British occupation — there was commerce going on. And the same unflagging diligence on the part of many of the same people after the peace rebuilt the ravaged port. It sent vessels to India and tall ships to Cathay and salesmen to the hinterlands, sweeping New York in a few short decades to first place among American seaport cities.

South Street Museum's interest in the revolutionary years lies less in the great pattern of history than in the simple threads of its fabric, and in the lives of people who lived its days. Through them we see not what happened, but what the happenings meant. And we glimpse, through the minutiae of daily lives, a little of the collective single-minded energy that built the magnificence of the 19th century seaport we are coming to know today.

E. F. R.

1

A Tentative Peace

1763

It was 1763, and peace was in the air. A war was over between England and France — a war that had been as courtly as a minuet, and made good talk across the tables of the coffee-houses. King George's War had brought fortune to some New York merchants in the form of military provisioning contracts. And to everyone's delight, there were soldiers on the streets with pay in their pockets, and they'd seemed "exceedingly public Spirited in the consumption of strong liquor." The prodigious quantities of rum and bread, meat and wine those men consumed had kept warehouses filled, and kept vessels on the water, running up and down the coast and out to the Caribbean islands to bring in cargo after cargo of provisions.

A young Scottish mariner named Joseph Rose had been part of all this. He was 28 years old in 1763, and though the details of his life at this point are obscure, it's likely that most of his time was passed at sea as a crew member on the coastal trading sloop *Industry,* whose trips to southern ports at Charleston and Virginia could have furnished supplies to a merchant who held one of the provision contracts.

Up and down the coast the gloriously named *Industry* worked, carrying flour and rum and bread, perhaps, and apples, cheese and barrel-staves out of New York. Then she'd return with South Carolina's purple indigo and low-country rice and Virginia's brown tobacco. At Philadelphia, Virginia, Charleston and Antigua there were men of the Rose family, probably distant relatives, who formed a kind of commercial network making things simple and orderly for the New York mariners. Everything was organized, dependable, profitable — and completely unspectacular.

Other vessels made even more profitable trips to the West Indies islands in the warm waters of the Caribbean, carrying provisions, livestock and re-exported European luxuries out to the sugar-cane planters whose vast, slave-tended estates were so profitable that not an

9

From the grassy summit of an uptown hill New York looks peacefully distant in the quiet of 1763. Madison Street bisects this place today, and by 1794 the harbor-edge city fringes extended nearly this far north. (See the view on page 58 to measure 31 years of growth.) The L-shaped house facing the East River is the Rutgers mansion, and the little steep-roofed building (right foreground) is a brew-house reached by a narrow path called Love Lane (I. N. Phelps Stokes Collection, New York Public Library).

acre could be spared for food crops. In return, New York ships filled their holds with molasses and rum, crudely refined sugar and a few limes or a stack of good, aged mahogany. Officially, New York ships went only to the British West Indies and a few other places, but as England knew, those enterprising shipmasters sailed openly into every Caribbean port they could get to under the white flag of truce. There is therefore "little distinction," complained a Boston paper of this flagrant law-flaunting, "between a merchant and a smuggler."

Enforcement of the century-old act prohibiting trade with foreign colonies was so negligible as to be unimportant, and by 1763 the economic balance of New York and the other colonial ports depended on cash from the foreign islands in return for supplies — and innumerable colonial rum-distillers needed more molasses than they could possibly get from the legal trade alone. Since England had winked at the law for so long, the colonials had "become reconciled to [smuggling] by example, habit and custom, and have gradually consented to amuse themselves with some very superficial arguments

10

in its favor, such as, that every man has the natural right to exchange his property with whom he pleases . . ."

Far more interesting than smuggling (at least to those who read of it in the newspapers!), and far more dangerous to those involved, was privateering. Political piracy, it really was: the armed capture of enemy ships. Since a ship captured that way became the property of the privateer's owner, cargo and all, the gains that could be made were staggering. So tempting was the lure of piracy that in 1758 New York Governor De Lancey wrote to London "that the country was drained of many able-bodied men by almost a madness to go a-privateering." Isaac Sears earned his first notoriety as the commander of a privateer. Rude and swashbuckling and intelligent, not a moment of peace in his personal history, Sears was the son of a New England oyster catcher. Nearly devoid of polish and property, he'd been bred up to the sea. At age 27, in command of the *Harlequin,* Sears and his crew attacked a French ship in the Spanish Main. He lost the ship (and nine of his men) but discovered his own peculiar genius for leadership. Isaac Sears made no fortune privateering, but he did earn quite enough to settle down on shore as a shopkeeper around 1763.

Placed higher than Sears in the ranks of city merchants was Isaac Low. Distinguished of family and station, just Rose's age, Low was an indifferent businessman who'd recently married into the landed Cuyler

11

family. Few people knew that he was a grandson of the late 17th century radical Jacob Leisler, but that did not really matter. Much of the stately grace of New York mercantile life on its highest level was his, and he kept his counting-house in fashionable Hanover Square and lived in a four-story brick house set aristocratically behind a gate on Dock Street (today's Pearl Street just above Coenties Slip). At 28, Low was already a member of the city's mercantile elite.

Joseph Rose himself, whose only entry into public notice was through an occasional custom-house report, is in some ways more interesting than his prominent neighbors. Reading of the revolutionary years today, we see them dominated by people like Sears and Low. In reality, though, the years belonged much more to people who lived as

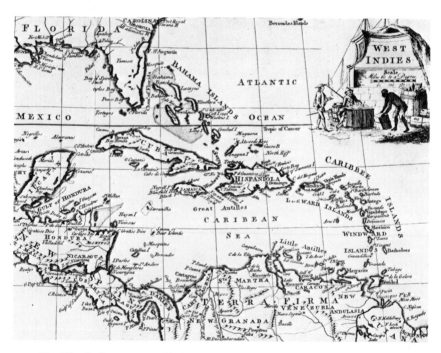

The West Indies meant wealth for colonial merchants whose provision-laden ships worked down the stormy Atlantic coast to island sugar ports. The goods they brought back — thick brown molasses and muscovado sugar — fed profitable rum distilleries in Northern cities. Captain Joseph Rose of Industry *out of New York traded in the Windward Islands (lower right) and later specialized in the lumber trade on Honduras Bay (left) and the Mosquito Shore (Map Division, New York Public Library).*

12

Joseph Rose did — quietly. Descended obscurely (if romantically) through a series of younger sons, Rose's ancestors probably came from the Scottish highlands near Inverness, whence the man presumed to be his father, a Jacobite supporter of Bonnie Prince Charlie, fled to America with his 10-year old son in 1745. In 1763 Joseph was a mariner. Thus, throughout the years of ferment, he was away from New York more than he was at home; and he wanted nothing more than the chance to grow comfortably prosperous living a good and peaceful life.

It was late in 1763 when England's confirmed peace with France brought an end to New York's halcyon days of easy trade and sudden fortune. For the first time, Great Britain turned critical attention to the merchants' half-concealed smuggling — with disastrous results. Colonial customs officials — many of whom had been given their jobs as political plums, and had never even been to North America — were ordered to their posts, and suddenly the West Indies trade lost most of its appeal. Hard money dwindled to almost nothing, merchants failed, distillers went dry, and laborers found themselves without work. With the war over there were no more supply contracts, and no more privateering to be done. "Everything is tumbling down," someone mourned then, "even the Traders." And on those traders the very well-being of the city depended.

The worst was still to come. The next April a Sugar Act confirmed the impossible situation the West Indian merchants found themselves in — while lowering the stated duty (import tax) on molasses from the British islands, the act made it very clear that the duties would now actually be collected. (Heretofore, enterprising captains could find ways to land molasses without paying duties.) The act also reinforced the exorbitant duties on imports from the sugar islands belonging to foreign countries, in effect prohibiting the trade that had sustained many leading merchants.

Joseph Rose was not seriously affected by the vigilance or the Sugar Act. Nor was Isaac Low, who dealt in upstate furs and European goods. And Isaac Sears had no great fortune invested in illicit West Indian trade, although he may have been professionally interested in it. The three men, though, could not have escaped being affected by the general symptoms of depression that were beginning to show. Rose, for example, reaching port with a cargo of South Carolina rice, might have had more difficulty selling it in 1764 than in 1763.

The regulatory laws kept on coming, inexorably, all through the year. One embarrassed the colonies by forbidding them to make their own paper money. Another forbade their settling west of the Appalachians. Then came the burdensome Quartering Act, commanding each colony to raise public revenue to house and feed all the British soldiers stationed in it.

Within the course of a single year the seed of discontent had been sown and it had germinated. No city had fared better than New York on the lucrative contracts and benign neglect of King George's War, and no city found its style more cramped by the Acts of 1764. "Our Spirits [are] sunk to as low an Ebb, as by natural Consequences our Purses must be bye and bye . . ."; and by wintertime, in a city recently described as almost vulgarly delighted with its own wealth, the papers were full of praise for little domestic economies. Simple funerals . . . sassafras, balm and sage teas . . . homespun cloth . . . twice-turned trousers.

It was in this mood of smoldering indignation that the city listened to tales and rumors that worse was still to come.

Merchant seamen leisurely supervise goods-stowing at a West Indies port. One (center background) checks a cargo manifest, but his friends are about to sample the local product — rum. The gently crumbling warehouse is filled with rum- or sugar-barrels — see the tremendous size of the one blocking the door. Out on the wharf a sturdy three-legged scale weighs a massive cask as a native rolls another toward it (detail, 1784 map, Map Division, New York Public Library).

2

Merchants
and the
Sons of Liberty

1764–1766

In the bitter gray days at the end of the winter of 1764–65, New York merchants began to watch for the deep-laden ships bringing spring goods from England. Warehouse floors were swept clean, boarding-house beds were plumped and sheeted, new clerks were hired and run ragged in preparation for one of the year's two great business seasons. These were frantic times for the merchants. There were hardly enough days to get the new goods stowed before the first of the country store-buyers were on the roads and upon them.

In other years the merchants must have taken delight in the cargoes their ships brought in. The English goods were the ones everyone talked about, they were literally the spice of life and the trappings of polite society. Colonial life would be unthinkable without them, and some of them are our proudest heirlooms today — shimmering bolts of the finest cloth, ribbons and lace for fancy dresses. Fragrant China tea and shell-thin porcelain delicately painted in cobalt and gold. Richly carved tables and chairs and delicate gilded mirrors. Dark cocoa, pungent spices, foreign wines. From trading nations all over the globe the world's manufactures and natural treasures had poured into English ports for re-export to the colonies. For as colonies, the Americans were permitted these imports only through England. Thus far the arrangement had worked well for everyone concerned.

The West Indies goods figured in the spring season too (but they were generally overshadowed by the impressive European arrivals). At the end of January, for example, the Rose sloop *Industry,* held up by ice in the harbor for several weeks, sailed for the Windward Islands with a host of other vessels. They'd begin to trickle back, one by one and two by two, in late March and April.

In this February of 1765, though, the English ships brought dread-

The hateful stamps.

ful news with the early spring goods, and it's easy to guess that the merchants left the gazing and checking and stowing to their clerks as they gathered, troubled, in Wall Street and the coffee-houses. A Stamp Act was before the King. Its passage would force Americans to pay a revenue tax to go about all sorts of ordinary jobs: clearing vessels out of the harbor, printing newspapers, vending spiritous liquors . . . even getting married! Without the representation in Parliament that British subjects "at home" enjoyed, the Americans were being taxed. On the floor of Parliament, one man warned that the radical American "Sons of Liberty" were not willingly going to tolerate the new Act . . .

But the King approved the Act in March, and from letters written from England to government officials and merchants, American newspapers pieced out the story. The stamps were coming, and by the first of November their use would be required.

"This Government continues in perfect Tranquillity," recorded Lieutenant-Governor Cadwallader Colden with anxious optimism. But the merchants, unable to overcome Sugar Act difficulties, suffered "frequent Bankruptcys." Commerce was so bad that "the grass [was] growing in . . . most trading streets."

Feeling at a disadvantage for living on the wrong shore of the Atlantic, the American merchants were still proudly certain that they could make Parliament see their side. So they set about stirring up "those whom [some] call the Mob and [others] the Sons of Liberty" to make a show of unified dissatisfaction for the benefit of the London merchants and their government supporters.

Stores and streets and taverns buzzed during the hot, unhappy months of summer 1765. Isaac Sears, restive and probably a little bored with the quiet life of a merchant after the years at sea, had turned the full force of his attention to politics. Although he was never the intellectual leader of popular protest, he was the man who could rally the Mob. With renewed delight in the powers of his own talk, he drew crowds to his father-in-law's tavern at the head of Beekman Slip (near the present corner of Fulton and Pearl streets). "The Public papers [are] crammed with Treason," complained one Englishman. And soon the merchant appointed to dispense the stamps resigned, fearful for the safety of "Person and Fortune."

On October seventh, three weeks before the Stamp Act became effective, delegates from nine of the 13 colonies held the Stamp Act Congress in New York's old City Hall. The men dispatched a formal statement of protest to their government. It went unheeded.

At Burns City Tavern the merchants planned a boycott. Forgivably over-rating the importance to the British merchants of their trade, they decided on a dignified refusal to purchase goods from England until tax and restrictions were removed. Sears, though, had other ideas regarding protest, and they were less stately than the boycott. The rambunctious faction of the city was in high spirits. For the time being, the lovers of quiet and peace receded behind doors while the Sons of Liberty "trampouzed" the streets with lanterns and song. A young boy

Romantically ramshackle, as it looked 40 years after the Revolution, this 18th century gristmill at West Farms on the Bronx River is typical of hundreds of mills that sent flour downriver to be shipped out from New York port (Museum of the City of New York).

from a town on the banks of the Hudson "had the good luck to get on Board a sloop from Claverack," on which he arrived at New York November first "like hell out of a Great Gun" ready for excitement.

The demonstration that was staged that dark and windless night that the Stamp Act took effect was absolutely masterful. With no bloodshed at all the Lieutenant-Governor was burned in effigy, his coach was stolen from under the very muzzles of loaded cannon, the house of the pompous British Major James was looted and sacked; then, in the words of the boy from Claverack, "all Peacable the mob went . . . every man to his home."

Noisy as these months were, there were people in the city who kept on about the business of their lives. Joseph Rose must have known that the stamps would affect him when the first of November arrived, but until then there were still cargoes to get that were legal and duty-free, and business (though not "as usual") would go on. Up and down the coast *Industry* ran, loading rice and indigo, cotton and tobacco at little tidewater docks where politics had nothing to do with everyday life. Only once a month, for about a week, do the shipping news columns show that Rose was back at the New York waterfront, and then he was hard at work at his job: off-loading the barrels and bales of his cargo, vending it and taking on a new one. As a coasting sloop, *Industry* could well have been berthed near Beekman's Slip, or Peck's, and it's a likely guess that Rose saw or heard Isaac Sears as he stalked through the muddy streets toward Drake's waterfront tavern late in the afternoon. Staunch, Scottish Rose, though, kept on trading. He apparently cared far more for the tangible fruits of *Industry* than for the ethereal joys of Liberty.

Isaac Low (and other well-born merchants with him) was fully committed to working for the repeal of the Sugar and Stamp acts, certain that trade would soon be back on its old course. Isaac Sears was committed too, and he had never been so absorbingly involved in things before.

It was late in November 1765 that 1200 New Yorkers met to authorize a petition to the Assembly, insisting that the Stamp Act be ignored. "It has no Force," the men agreed, "but what we give it." Afterward, on every side, the city began to resume a little of its life. Newspapers had already been printed without the stamps, and now vessels sailed gaily out of the harbor without stamped let-passes. "The

Stamp Act repeal is celebrated in this British cartoon funeral of Miss Americ-Stamp while port-city warehouses let down crates of goods bound for the colonies. These English warehouses with open ground floors and exterior cargo hoists that extend over the water are more advanced technically than the New York merchants' small brick house-and-shops (Prints Division, New York Public Library).

Merchants in this place think they have a right to every freedom of Trade which the Subjects of Great Britain enjoy," observed Cadwallader Colden correctly. And "people in general are averse to Taxes of any kind." The winter passed in defiance and proud adherence to the boycott. And then in May 1766 came word that the Stamp Act had been repealed, and the tariff on British West Indian molasses was reduced to a negligible penny per gallon.

"Joy to America!" was emblazoned in the New York *Mercury.* The boycott had been successful, the merchants thought, though loss of their trade hadn't been as hard on England as they'd hoped. Toasts were drunk in the taverns, and indomitable Sears led a rejoicing band of "Inhabitants" aboard a merchantman at the docks and seized "strong beer and ale in Bottles and English cheese from England!" The first of the red-capped liberty poles was set up on the Common, and "the Night ended in drunkenness," an official wrote wearily.

Good days were back again, and the city basked in a growing prosperity. Joseph Rose, with nothing more to stand in the way of his happiness, married Barbary Egburson. New York's Assembly voted money for a stone statue to honor William Pitt, who had convinced

19

Parliament "that the Stamp Act should be repealed absolutely, totally and immediately," and in an access of good feeling also ordered a gilt lead image of George III on horseback.

"No more meetings of the Sons of Liberty," recorded Captain John Montresor in obvious relief. "No more caballing and Committees at every corner of the Street."

But temporarily overlooked, or at least ignored in the joy of the day, were several factors that would make trouble later. One was the continuation of the duty on imported rum and sugar: Parliament thus claimed its right to levy an unapproved tax on the colonies. Another was the Declaratory Act, passed on the day the Stamp Act was repealed, asserting that Parliament could make laws binding the American colonists "in all cases whatsoever." Third was the presence of restless soldiers, quartered in town without the consent of the citizens. The final concern was the newly mobilized Sons of Liberty, who took their own interest in Parliament's reprehensible Acts, and whose rumbustious doings, it was now clear, were not subject to regulation by their well-to-do, conservative neighbors. The disaster of war itself was postponed by the Stamp Act repeal, but tension remained. Thoughtful men knew, even in this respite, that trouble still lay ahead.

Friends often met at the street-corner pumps in early New York. Family members came there to draw wash-water, and at summer dusk nearby street lamps drew children from houses the way they do today. Here the "old Watch House wench" peddles hot corn to a well dressed passerby, and the long-handled pump awaits use (from a painting by William P. Chappel, ca. 1805, Museum of the City of New York).

3
On the
Way to War
1767–1769

It was then that money began to flow in all sorts of channels," wrote Mrs. Lamb, a 19th century historian whose own grandparents could have recalled these times. "Riches, long hoarded, came into prominent view. Houses were built with the rapidity of magic, . . . merchants patched extensions up on their warehouses or built new ones, every thing old was mended, and fresh paint took a mad race through the length and breadth of the town."

Cash was still short, though, more goods were imported than exported, and the balance of trade was unfavorable to colonial merchants. Then, in summer 1767, news came from England of the Townshend Act, which placed new duties on a long list of everyday things: tea, window glass, paper, painters' colors . . . While Bostonians rioted, New Yorkers virtuously smuggled, evading the tax wherever possible. "Whole Cargoes from Holland and Ship Loads of Wine" were smuggled in by many an enterprising merchant, and the prevailing spirit favored the revival of illegal trade.

But smuggling alone wasn't the answer to this latest blow to trade. A second boycott was soon planned, and although competing port-city Philadelphia refused to cooperate, New York's importers adopted a set of resolutions that would curtail their own trade in protest. The goal was the complete removal of unapproved import duties, and the return of commerce to the comfortable situation it was in before 1764. Isaac Low headed a committee formed to keep careful watch against unwelcome imports filtering into the city by land or sea, especially from Philadelphia, whose merchants accepted British goods well into 1769; and from Boston, whose merchants were justly suspected by New Yorkers of smuggling English things.

Throughout 1769 New Yorkers were determined to bring about what they considered to be fair treatment by the government. In resolutions they affirmed the common British birthright of being represented in Parliament before being taxed, the right to petition for redress of grievances, and the right of their own provincial legislatures to certain local powers. Yet time and again contemporary accounts confirm continuing loyalty to the King. A ship named *Brittania* went down the ways at an East River shipyard with her figurehead "expressive of our invariable Affection for . . . the Chief of Nations."

Joseph Rose, proud of his hard-earned title of "Captain," now had become a man of some substance. Late in 1769, with 31 other shipmasters, he sat in the long upper room of the Broad Street exchange to hammer out a draft for the charter of a Marine Society. Its purpose was noble and certainly innocent: to promote maritime knowledge and to protect members' wives and children. Yet one man could suspect even this peaceable group of encouraging "the Wantonness of the Populace."

In the spring of 1769 the three great American ports had finally united in non-importation of British goods, but violations were rife, and merchants, who had the most to lose by the agreement, were

Both of these churches were new in 1768 — the Brick Presbyterian Church on Park Row (center) was begun when cash began to flow after the Stamp Act repeal, and St. Paul's Chapel, New York's oldest church today, was completed in 1766.

22

After the Stamp Act was passed Americans began to look for ways to replace imported goods with things of their own manufacture. This air furnace for casting iron was built in 1767 for Peter Curtenius & Company. The firm made hardware for local use: tea kettles, pots, stoves, plows and other items of domestic utility (courtesy of the New-York Historical Society).

obviously tired of sacrifice. It was, after all, hard on men like Isaac Low, whose store was usually full of expensive European goods, to do little business while men like Joseph Rose went on making slow but steady money on trading with other colonial ports.

Patience was wearing thin.

Seventeen-seventy was rung in with a riot that must have satisfied even Sears. Some garrisoned soldiers had made an attack on the liberty pole, thus arousing the partisans who had put it up. Tension between soldiers and citizens had been growing steadily, and on the 19th of January there was a confrontation on Golden Hill (John Street today, between Burling Slip and Cliff Street) after more of the soldiers were caught nailing up an insulting placard that began with a poem:

> God and a soldier, all Men doth adore,
> In Time of War and not before;
> When the War is over, and all Things righted,
> God is forgotten and the Soldier slighted.

From all over the commercial district, men had run from their work, clutching as weapons whatever came to hand. Michael Smith, a young cabinetmaker's apprentice, recalled having the turned leg of a chair gripped club-like in his hand. "We are all confusion," a man wrote to a London friend when it was all over. "The Soldiers have . . . blowed up the Liberty Pole," and though no one died "much Blood was spilt." "Liberty is the pretext," wrote one merchant in disgust. "But, it may be interpreted thus; if we cannot breed a Disturbance . . . in one Way, we must in another."

The incomplete repeal of the Townshend duties in April cast the

New York's East River shipyards were her proudest industry: the sleek and speedy vessels that went down the ways there did justice to the English flag. Up in the tall-roofed lofts of some of the waterfront buildings (above), sailmakers stitched great white widths of canvas for the wind-ships. Seated on the special bench that holds his marlin-spikes, mallet and twine, this 18th century craftsman works up a seam. Christian Bergh's shipyard (below), shown years after the Revolution ended, is at work. A light-frocked laborer rests on the spar from which he has just released his team, and to his left a wooden figurehead leans on a fence. The black iron cauldron holds pitch for caulking the vessel's seams (sailmaker, Steel, Elements and Practice of Rigging; shipyard painting by William P. Chappel, 1809, Museum of the City of New York).

Opposite: ship details from a 1774 cartoon (courtesy of the New-York Historical Society).

24

city into a ferment, and while cherry trees flowered in the Out Ward fields, the people were "run mad with Faction and party; not in defense of our Common Right, but against each other . . ." Parliament had asserted its controversial power against the colonies by retaining the tax on tea. But the lean years had been hard and England had dangled a tempting lure. Isaac Low's latest advertisement in the *Mercury* had been dismal — it featured "a small parcel of old coat," and other merchants had tried to make enticing "rare and secret herb cures" and "a few left over blue and white China plates." They wanted very badly to end the boycott and order English goods again (except for the still-taxed items), while the noisy radicals purposed to hold out for the total repeal of the duties.

Meetings, polls, midnight visits and streetcorner committees again: broadsides and accusations. But early in July the *Earl of Halifax* glided inevitably out of the harbor for Falmouth, with orders for "a general importation of Goods" aboard her, "except the single article, TEA . . ." The merchants had carried the day, but in doing so they'd split with the Sons of Liberty, who considered the goods-ordering "a sordid and wanton defection" by a set of greedy traders. Gradually, and after they permitted themselves innumerable insulting letters to New York, the merchants of the other big seaports resumed normal commerce, and the brief years that followed were ones of relative prosperity and apparent tranquillity.

So it was to be, for a few more years. Ferment and respite, radical agitations and conservative soothings; all building up tensions that would soon become unbearable.

From Philadelphia

From N-York

4
Days of Grace
1770–1773

No one could have lived in New York in 1770 unaware that the colonies were in crisis. But even Isaac Sears saw ships in the harbor, saw sailmakers at work, went into open shops. Politics claimed the forefront, but there were countless people who left protest to others, preferring to go on as they could with the work they knew best.

Captain Rose was one of those steadfast men: perhaps he'd seen too much of protest in Scotland, or more likely he just cared more for *Industry*, Barbary, and his young children Joseph and William than he did for politics. By 1770 Rose was sailing a sturdy new brig he'd named *Industry* after the older sloop. Capacious and steady, *Industry* could make the run south to the West Indies and the Spanish Main in about a month. Frequently his trips took him through the Windward Passage between Cuba and Hispaniola to the English logging camps on Honduras Bay and the Mosquito Shore. There he'd load mahogany planks for New York's skilled cabinetmakers, and logwood for black and purple inks and dyes. Between trips, now that he had his own vessel to load and maintain, and a family to claim willing attention, Captain Rose often found himself at home for two months at a time. He hired draymen to heave logs and sacks and barrels from *Industry's* hold, conferred with merchants about exports and orders, visited distilleries to watch his muscovado turned to rum. The work of Rose's seaport days was profitable, absorbing and familiar.

It was about this time that Joseph and Barbary must have started planning the house they wanted. There had to be a place for a shop — Joseph would one day retire from the sea and start a business of his own — and there had to be a place to store the crated cargoes from *Industry* and the other vessels from which Joseph would buy goods. Typical houses the Roses saw in New York as they thought about their own were two or three stories high with handsome pitched or gambrel roofs and wood cornices painted white. The best houses were built of brick, and others, built of wood, had brick fronts. Window lintels, stoops and trim were often made of the chocolate-colored brownstone quarried locally.

If the Roses built on the waterfront, there would be a wharf at the back for *Industry,* and extra income from wharfage rented to other vessels. A Water Street lot was thus desirable, but in 1771 with merchants building anew as they never had before, wharfed real estate was gaining in value every day. Newly filled land beyond Peck's Slip, however, wasn't prohibitive yet. After all, nothing had been built there and only the country boats with foods for the Peck's Slip market came to the piers. But the city was steadily growing northward along its east shore, and even as the Roses watched in 1771, docks and landfill were replacing the boat-houses that used to stand behind the tall-roofed mansions on St. George's Square. (Pearl Street's block between Peck's Slip and Dover Street.)

Home from Honduras in the first brisk days of fall in 1771, Captain Rose could have seen the advertisement on the back sheet of the *Mercury.* Two lots for sale — already docked — on Water Street behind William Walton's house. The place was next to an old blacksmith shop

Troubled New York knew uneasy peace between 1769 and 1773, and in those days of grace men gladly went back to their old jobs and joys. Here on a peaceful day while the respite lasted, a handsome frigate lies moored off the west shore of Manhattan and 13 men pull past in a rowboat (detail, 1773 print, Museum of the City of New York).

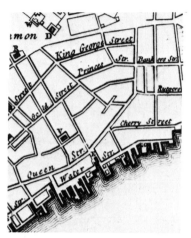

In a trim and speedy brig like the one shown above left, named Industry, *Captain Joseph Rose sailed to the West Indies and the Spanish Main for about a decade after 1770. When he began to think of settling down on shore in a house of his own, Rose bought a Water Street building lot just above Peck Slip (see map upper right). It was a convenient spot for a mariner — he could moor* Industry *at his own backyard dock, and rent the wharf to others when out of port himself (brig from Steel,* Elements and Practice of Rigging; *map detail, 1780, Eno Collection, New York Public Library).*

one of the Waltons used for ship repairs, and there was a wash-water pump across the street. By the middle of October Rose had bought the land. Edward Laight, a hardware dealer who already had a shop nearby on Queen Street, owned the second lot, and the two families may have built together, with a "gangway" passing between their houses to the backyards and the river.

Shipping news reported in the *Mercury* shows that Joseph Rose was in New York more than usual through the fair months of 1772, and it's easy to imagine him walking out often on Water Street, unpaved past Peck's Slip, to the place where workmen were digging his cellar-hole and lining it with rough hewn stones from the fields. Later, skilled craftsmen would frame out and sheath the walls, working deftly with heavy tools and lumber. Windows and doors took definite form, and when the long, rough rafters were pegged into place, the structure began to look like a house.

In March of 1773 Captain Rose advertised that he had rooms to let in the "very convenient house . . . he now lives in, near Peck's Slip." Late that summer, a neighbor's advertisement mentioned "Captain Rose and Mr. Laight's new dock." Rose, who had never been politically involved, now found himself sharing a wharf with a man who had. It's impossible for us to know how friendly he was with Edward Laight, but

Joseph Rose's neighborhood, seen from across the East River around 1796, is one of small waterfront houses, backyard wharfs and seaport activity. The gambrel-roofed mansion just right of center is the Walton House, and the three-story building far right may be Edward Laight's house, Joseph Rose's next-door neighbor (detail, pantographic view of the City of New York from Brooklyn Heights by C. B. J. F. de St. Memin, 1796; copy by M. Dripps, ca. 1850).

This worn and battered four-story building incorporates the surviving elements of Joseph Rose's house and shop. It may not be the building of 1773, but one that replaced it some years later. A disastrous fire in 1904 burned much of the 18th century building, but the second floor facade and a bit of the ground floor appear to be original, as are the rough stone walls of the old cellar beneath it (photograph by Edmund V. Gillon, Jr.).

if they talked at all, they spoke of the day's issues, and Laight must have told Rose about the hectic time he'd had the year before working for the re-establishment of English trade. Laight's political associates were the moderates: Isaac Low spoke for the faction, and Laight was often with his neighbors William and Abraham Walton, nephews of the merchant prince who lived in the mansion on the Square. In later years Abraham Walton built a store on the other side of Laight's, and Joseph Rose had these involved, moderate men as neighbors.

They all wanted to get business back on course, and Rose knew as well as they did that England's naval protection was indispensable to safe and happy trade. All Laight's circle had opposed the Stamp Act (Laight himself had protested with the Sons of Liberty in 1765), and none of them had approved of the Townshend duties. But they were confident in the power of American boycott, and believed that the remaining taxes would soon be lifted.

One can imagine these men, met for an evening of cards and punch,

Trinity's steeple dominates built-up New York in 1773, and sloping downhill behind the church, little house-lined streets run to the North River wharfs. This is the 18th century's one good illustration of what wharfs looked like as men framed them out and filled them right behind merchants' houses (detail, 1773 print, Museum of the City of New York).

The best water New Yorkers could get came from the tea-water pump at the corner of Park Row and Roosevelt Street. Fed by the Collect Pond, it gave sweeter water than people could get from their own, or the street-corner pumps. Here a peddler starts his rounds — he's filled the cask on his specially built cart, and he'll measure water for customers in the leather bucket he carries (from a painting by William P. Chappel, 1807, Museum of the City of New York).

Eighteenth century men talk on the Governor's Island beach while a little dog romps on the sand. Through dialogue and debate, by twos, by threes and by scores, people formed and strengthened their opinions on the day's issues before the Revolution much as they do today (detail, Ratzer map, 1767, New York Public Library).

smoking thoughtfully in their blue and brown cloth jackets, blouses white in the candlelight and nankin trousers tight at the knees. They may even have met sometimes in Joseph Rose's fine little Water Street house.

Of Isaac Sears (by then called "King"), whom all of them may have known through their common connection with Trinity Church, they were critical. Moderates deplored the "fondness for bawling out the word freedom, and sporting with liberty colors, liberty caps, and liberty poles" he was imparting to an ever more arrogant, shifting, expanding group of "Inhabitants" who seemed ready to spend half the night

31

In December 1773 the Boston "Mohawks" made history with some cases of tea in a way Americans never forgot (see detail above left), but this cartoon shows that not all of their activities were so harmless. The man in duck feathers is an excise collector: his tormentors are punishing him as a symbol for Parliament's tax on tea and the monopoly they granted a British tea company (courtesy of the New-York Historical Society).

shouting through the streets on any pretext at all. "Flaming patriots without property," others called them. "Liberty Boys. A set that was all absurdity."

Laight and his friends had sensed, when they were ready to end the boycott in 1770, that the "Inhabitants" under the leadership of four or five active and articulate men, were becoming a force apart from the moderate protesters, and one they could not ignore. And they were uneasy, for recently there'd been whisperings and rumors come down from New England, and taken up in the taverns along the waterfront. The "Inhabitants" were hearing new definitions of "liberty," they were being shown that even if the colonies were represented in Parliament, only the wealthy Americans would be heard, for they alone could vote. Now, in a republic, every man votes . . .

The peaceful times of 1771 and 1772 were as short and as doomed as the days of grace before winter storms, and by the middle of 1773 they were gone. Parliament had granted England's foundering East India Company, tea merchants, the right to export to America, paying duties themselves in hopes that a market could be tempted. Sears and the other radical leaders emerged from three years of unwilling retirement, and "A new Flame is apparently Kindling in America," a diarist wrote, "and now the Sons of Liberty and the Dutch [tea] smugglers set up the Cry of Liberty."

Philadelphia, Boston and New York had tea-ships on the way, and the reception one of them got in Boston harbor on the 16th of December is American legend. Throughout the winter the Mechanics (for so the "Inhabitants" began to call themselves) kept vigil against the arrival of New York's tea-ships, and one following the other they were sighted in April 1774. But they never landed, for Sears had concocted for them a tea party of their own.

Joseph Rose had come in from Honduras before the tea party, and he could have heard the guarded anxiousness his moderate friends expressed over it, but he'd cleared out again before the incredible news came early in May. The King had shut the port of Boston.

Isaac Sears at a coffee-house, drawn from imagination in 1882.

5
City of War
1774–1776

A queasy calm hung over docks and streets and shops in New York as it came to be spring 1774. No one could ignore what was going on by the light of whale-lamps glimpsed behind blear-paned windows on waterfront alleys. Edward Laight going from his store to Murray's Wharf or the coffee-house late in an afternoon, surely must have seen rough-coated figures hurrying toward Drake's door; heard, as he passed, the ardor in King Sears' voice as it rose and fell, accusing, confiding, commanding. "The mob begin to think and reason," a wealthy young man named Gouverneur Morris dispassionately observed. "The gentry begin to fear this."

When the British packet *Samson* arrived early that May the news she carried — the closing of Boston's port — exploded in the tensed city like a Roman candle. Behind shuttered windows Sears and the Mechanics fired off a secret letter to Boston while the merchants gasped with the realization that England could close New York as well. Justifiably fearful of what the Mechanics were likely to do the moderates trooped in force to a radicals' meeting that was described later by patriot Alexander McDougall. Packed to the walls and jammed in the hall outside a room that couldn't begin to hold them, men listened as Isaac Sears began to speak, beseechingly, of Boston. He wanted another boycott, but Low forced him deftly, while the aristocratic Walton brothers shouted, out of the limelight. Thus Low and the others, who had come to a radical meeting for conservative reasons, won the night. Instead of the furious denunciations and pledges of non-importation Sears had planned to wring from the crowd, a Committee was chosen to write a stately, rational letter to the Bostonians.

"The cause is general and concerns a whole continent," said Chairman Low's careful Committee-letter, and a general Convention of the colonies was arranged. Low went as a moderate to the First Continental Congress in September, but before long the radical delegates were calling for severance of trade with England and her

34

dependencies. ". . . Can the people bear a total interruption of the West India trade?" Low argued hopefully. "Can they live without rum, sugar and molasses? This would cut up revenue by the roots," he insisted, "if wine, fruit, molasses and sugar were discarded as well as tea." But he was overborne, and the new restrictions, called an "Association," went into force immediately.

Preliminaries dealt with, the Congress went on to matters even more disturbing to Low and the other New York delegates. Militias were to be formed, and royal officials ignored. Distressed, Low spoke to the delegates with a confidence he didn't feel. "We have too much reason in this Congress," he said, "to suspect that independency is aimed at." But he realized that in some way, it was at least thought of.

Reasonable New Yorkers had grown up knowing that their city was built on trade. Like a pillar at the center of the system was England (still "home" to them in speech), and England made everything possible.

In the rarified circles of New York's aristocracy, severance from "home" would shatter a courtly world of favoritism and prestige. But to uncounted numbers of middle-class traders, "independency" would be disaster. The very cornerstone of life in 1774 would be knocked away — trade would be ruined. The loss of English imports and the voracious West Indian market alone would finish countless merchants. Without

To Burns Coffee House on Broadway the Sons of Liberty would hurry when the day's work was done to hear Isaac Sears speak, or to talk over the day. Shown here nearly a century after those turbulent times, it's an inviting old building with a graceful Georgian doorway and a big back garden (Museum of the City of New York).

British naval protection, American ships on the high seas would fall prey to one set of pirates after another.

And if the merchants failed, what would happen to that great fraction of the city's population whose work supported trade? What would happen to the seamen, the shipbuilders, the draymen, caulkers, riggers and clerks? Little wonder, then, that most Sons of Liberty came from the ranks of the landsman-artisans: chairmakers, shoemakers, schoolmasters, bricklayers.

Down on the docks there were dismal days early in 1775 as the Association was vigilantly enforced. There were days when no ship moved at all, when the wind carried no shouts from stevedores or draymen, and the rhythmic slap of little waves on the wooden sides of a brig made a lonely sound to a merchant's ears.

A little trading was still going on. In April Joseph Rose was loading *Industry* with horses and chickens and Indian corn for the little ports on the Bay of Honduras and the Musquito Shore. But shortly before he left a post rider came wildly slogging through the muddy roads of April

In long shed-like buildings on the edges of town, New York cordwainers spun the endless rope the seaport city needed. Since splicing weakened rope, the best method was to make it in single lengths long enough for any rigging requirement.

The BRIG
INDUSTRY,
JOSEPH ROSE,
MASTER;

NOW lying at Murray's wharf, bound for the Weſt-Indies, Muſqueto ſhore, and the Bay of Honduras, will ſail in 10 or 12 days. For freight or paſſage apply to ſaid maſter on board ; who has for ſale, a quantity of choice

MAHOGANY and LOGWOOD;
And a FEW
SPANISH HIDES,
Which he will ſell on reaſonable terms.

The way that history's great events and people's daily lives are interwoven shows well in the history of this advertisement Joseph Rose placed in the Mercury *on March 27, 1775. The notice ran for about a month and a half. The April issue that carried the shattering news of battle at Lexington also ran this advertisement and Rose's angry notice that someone had stolen "18 fathom of cable" from* Industry's *deck. The May day he cleared out of the harbor for Honduras was the day on which the Second Continental Congress convened at Philadelphia.*

shouting that there had been armed fighting a little way from Boston, and 93 Americans had been killed. The worst had finally come.

The news of Lexington and Concord galvanized the town. Sears pried his way into an armory and began to distribute muskets. "The armed citizens," noted radical Marinus Willett, "were constantly parading about the city without any Definite object," and the Committee of Observation was enlarged to a Committee of Safety twice its old size. Cabinetmaker Gilbert Ash, whose exquisite Chippendale furniture makes museums proud today, carried a musket in New York that summer, and so did a distiller named Nicholas Rose, perhaps a cousin to Joseph.

Imagine the city as it was, then, as summer came on in 1775. What peace could there be for anyone, with citizens ranging the streets with guns, and government in the hands of an emergency Committee? This was the climate Joseph Rose sailed away from on the eighth of May, and on the eighth of May in Philadelphia a second Congress seated itself to consider the latest news. It seated itself without Isaac Low, however, for even at New York's preliminary convention Low saw that the radicals were stronger than the moderates, and he knew that he could expect little success in "opposing measures of violence." The reconciliation he had worked for was out of the question now, and in disgust Low retired to his country house at Kings Bridge, in the woods to the north of town.

After this the moderates kept to themselves. "Hardly a tory face to

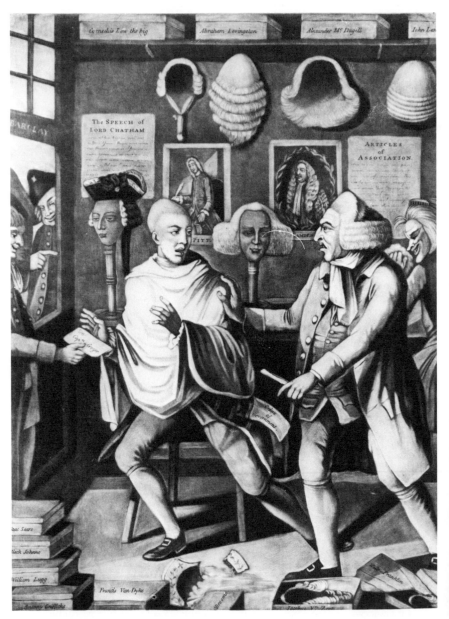

*The "patriotick barber of New York" angrily ejects from his premises — half shaved —
the captain of a British ship in the harbor. Spring and summer 1775 were hard times
for obvious British sympathizers — the ungentle Sons of Liberty carried the day. Wig-
boxes are labeled with the names of prominent radicals — Isaac Sears' box tops the stack
on the floor (I. N. Phelps Stokes Collection, New York Public Library).*

From the "sweet situation" Mrs. Walton enjoyed at Horn's Hook, dangerous Hell Gate was wild and beautiful scenery across which she could look to Manhattan's shore (Museum of the City of New York).

be seen" in June, but in August the fearsome great warship *Asia* loomed in the harbor, her cannon just visible from the city docks. In a terrifying reversal, the very navy that had protected the New Yorkers' ships in foreign waters now lay in the harbor with guns trained on their houses.

The days shortened, the air turned crisp and on every side New York was fortifying. *Asia* lay sullenly in the harbor, and her guns had boomed and killed in August. Certain that an attack on New York would follow the British evacuation of Boston, the revolutionary government concentrated such troops as it had in the city, and rough-clad militiamen were everywhere. They were a rude, disruptive force, and they turned the city upside down, fortifying, and sent families out of their houses. "You may recall a sweet situation at Horn's Hook," a townsman wrote of a house whose delightful order had been wrecked when the troops took it for defense. "When Mrs. Walton received the order to go out of her house she burst into tears, for she was fixed to her heart's content." There was grieving in the city as its people abandoned it sadly to defense.

"Every office is shut up," a leader of the radicals observed in November. "All business stagnated [and] the city half deserted for fear of a Bombardment. . ."

By the end of February 1776, the city streets were filled with American troops, some of them armed with nothing more than a fowling-piece or a scythe. Under the trees on the Common they wheeled and marched till the grass was ground to mud under their boots. A resident wrote of this uncomfortable time: "We are now a City of War."

39

Action and reaction flying across the ocean like a shuttlecock, England and her colonies were virtually in a state of war. Then: "ye Fleet has arrived here and lies in fair View of ye City" early in July, and "we Expect an Attack from the menwarr [sic] Every Moment."

Continental brigades were posted throughout the town: one company waited restlessly behind an embankment on the East River almost in sight of Joseph Rose's house. Life as it had been lived was clearly over, and now New Yorkers began to flee in earnest.

By early September nearly 20,000 people — four-fifths of the city's inhabitants — had abandoned their homes. Isaac Low had retreated under threat to New Jersey. Joseph Rose, if he hadn't left New York for safety before, doubtless took his family away now. Isaac Sears had gone back to his native Connecticut late in 1775, where he raised and led a troop of horsemen. Hard times, these were, for all. Rose, 41 years old

Mammoth British frigates Phoenix and Rose *worried fleeing New Yorkers who saw them from the Hudson River's banks as they passed in mid-August 1776. Brave rebels (left) try to ignite the enemy's vessels with a fire ship that billows smoke against the night sky. In detail above whaleboaters float on the luminous water eerily lit by the flames (I. N. Phelps Stokes Collection, New York Public Library).*

now, and just about ready to retire from the sea and build up a business at his store, left everything when he left Water Street. The store and *Industry,* worth together around £ 1,500, represented most of his capital. For the past 13 years, the best part of his adult life, he had been struggling against one political crisis after another for well-being. Now, with 130 men of war visible from his rear windows, he had to leave without knowing that there would even be a house on Rose's Wharf when he returned.

It was on the afternoon of the ninth of July 1776, that the Declaration of Independence was read aloud to troops and crowds who had expected the news for more than a month. There was joy on the streets that day, but quiet in their houses were families who believed that Congress was wrong.

A crush of celebrating "Inhabitants" with stout ropes pulled down

King George, the leaden equestrian, from his marble base on Bowling Green. Melted and re-formed into bullets of "molten Majesty" he'd be fired back at the King's own troops. But just more than a month later the Americans who had been so gay and proud in training returned, defeated on Brooklyn Heights, to a New York they would soon abandon. Then after them, in awful pursuit in 84 open boats, came the unbroken British ranks, their uniforms of brilliant color making them look to a country American "like a large clover-field in full bloom."

"The City of New York is now invaded by a powerful Fleet and Army," a New Yorker hastily scribbled on September second. "The Inhabitants are obliged to seek a Retreat in the Country." And for seven long years the British army occupied New York, and for seven long years more than half of the people who left that fall of 1776 were forced to stay away from their homes.

Inflamed by the news of independence, a celebrating crush of "Inhabitants" with stout ropes hauled the King's statue from its Bowling Green pedestal. Suggestively made of lead, the statue would soon become patriot bullets for firing at the King's own troops. No drawing was done at the time this happened, and the artist who made this woodcut in 1842 dressed the participants in 19th century clothes.

6
Garrison Town
1776–1783

In country towns along the Hudson River and little seaport villages exiled New Yorkers waited anxiously for news of their beleaguered city. To their waiting ears distressing reports came of red-coated men and dour gray ships, and worst of all came news of the fire that burnt 500 buildings in the densest part of town on September 21st. These must have been days of regret and longing for a way of life and a home that seemed to be forever gone.

But soon newspapers began to filter out from the city, and the exiles read of ships fitting out for England at the wharfs! And achingly, they saw the tempting advertisements of their townsmen who had stayed at home. New York papers hadn't carried notices like those for months. Rhinelander's store on Burling Slip had blue and white china bowls and looking glasses. The brig *Sukey* at Beekman's Slip had on board "Red Port wine, capers, sallad oyl and cordials." And silversmith Stephen Reeves was ready to get on with "business as usual." Joseph Rose could have seen distiller Richard Deane's list of goods, delectably headed by raspberry shrub, and thought of the thirsty soldiers who might have been his customers instead of Deane's.

There was trade in the city, and it looked like a haven to men of business who had no way to live and support their families outside it. To practical Joseph Rose, whose growing children (four sons and three daughters) needed shoes and shirts and dresses for oncoming winter, the urge to go on home prevailed. There had been nothing for a man like Rose to do outside the city, and before much time had passed he was back in his house on the wharf. Along his section of Water Street, at least, there was a reassuring number of familiar faces that fall, for Edward Laight was home too, and the Walton brothers, and Alexander Hamilton — not the famous lawyer, but a Scottish mariner-merchant who was Rose's friend. Life, though different from what it had been before the war, had begun again in New York. By December Isaac Low

A man like Rose who imported goods and groceries might have had shelves stocked like these with China tea, Madeira wine, Ceylon cinnamon and even more alluring imports. During the lean years of occupation, though, grocers' shelves were often painfully bare as the city awaited the arrival of its fleets of British victuallers.

Quiet in water that reflects the sun in a silver sheet, British frigates and merchant ships lie in New York harbor in 1778. Industry might be somewhere among the city's ships in this view (Museum of the City of New York).

was back at his Dock Street house, but Isaac Sears, devoted patriot, had gone to Boston to become a privateer.

By returning to their homes in New York, those families made a political statement whether they wanted to or not. By entering the city they put themselves under the King's protection, and the trade that would keep them fed was British. To New Yorkers who chose to stay away from their occupied city, the ones who'd returned were loyalists. But times of crisis look less like political history to people living through them than they do to people reading of them later, and in 1776 some people came home to garrison New York because there was safety and the chance to earn a living there.

"No man that is true to his country has any business there," remarked a rebel outside the lines, yet less than a third of the town's civilians signed a loyalist pledge, and first-hand accounts later implied that there was quiet joy in some quarters when the Paris peace treaty was signed in favor of America. Like Joseph Rose, many of the people who came into New York in 1776 stayed there after the peace to rebuild

45

the city and help it gain commercial brilliance during the last years of the 18th century.

That first winter of occupation was a gay and glittering time in contrast to the hard months that had gone before. The streets were bright with troops in blue and scarlet jackets, canary trousers, powdered heads and brass-trimmed caps, and in the stately houses and saloons tables were set with silver and spread with all the delicacies that Britain could ship and Long Island could grow. Trade fared well as merchants placed orders to go with the fleets that sailed in convoy to Cork and Glasgow, Bristol and London. British money fitted out loyalist privateers that swept the seas and brought prize after prize back to New York to be knocked down at the Wall Street auction blocks.

Joseph Rose began to call himself a merchant at last, and stacked his shelves to tempt the custom of the soldiers whose taste for European luxury wasn't satisfied by regulation stew and "baker's bread." Specializing as before in West Indian rums and sugars, he now began to advertise a full line of fancy grocer's goods: fruit brandy and madeira, chocolate, spices and tea. A sideline in little pleasantries distinguished him from other tradesmen — at his shop a man could find pipes and good tobacco, Rappee snuff and port, and a selection of shirt-buttons together with needles, thread and irons. For soldiers leaving on

The cartouche shown left, from a fireman's certificate of 1796, shows the awful emergency of fire in early New York. Fire fighting was dependent on volunteer companies with hand-pumped "engines" and citizen bucket brigades as illustrated here. While firemen and neighbors pour water into the burning buildings, occupants work with feverish haste to rescue valuable goods. In the detail above, a fire chief barks orders through a speaking trumpet as buckets pass hand to hand along the chain (Museum of the City of New York).

campaign he carried a stock of items he called "dispatches," guaranteed to cook a steak in four minutes, he said, "having made the tryal myself."

But just beneath the relief and bravado of occupied New York beat the grim rhythm of reality. Every day saw a soldier stalking the streets banging a tin pan before the overcrowded American prisons calling "Rebels turn out your dead."

While the houses of the lucky were bright with candles, the poor went "begging from house to house for sustenance." The conscience of the city spoke through Moravian reverend Ewald G. Schaukirk against such "great festivities . . . in . . . time of distress and calamity." And unforgettable through the seven years of occupation, the blackened, roofless walls of the buildings burnt in the 1776 fire stood unrepaired while the grimy canvas swags of squatters' shelters stretched and flapped between them.

When cold weather came in 1777 the rebel lines about New York pulled tighter and life was harder. It was difficult to get firewood and garden goods, and no one wanted to contemplate what might happen "should a Cork fleet miscarry," depriving the town of salt beef and pork, butter, cheese and even flour. "The markets are extreme bad," reported the papers again and again. Cash was scarce and food was costly, yet "many come to the town daily, so that it grows quite full."

In August 1778 a second fire began at a shipchandler's on Cruger's Wharf and ravaged nearly 100 buildings in the most crowded part of the city. The next afternoon a gun-powder ship exploded in the East River, blowing the east roof slopes off of houses on the waterfront streets and shattering windows. Joseph Rose's house must have been among the hardest hit by the blast.

"The inhabitants are most distressed," someone reported to a London newspaper, yet life went on, and sometimes happily. "We talk freely of politics," a man wrote of his impromptu club, "tell all the News, and are for the time happy." The Marine Society continued to meet, and the Chamber of Commerce was allowed to resume its work. Isaac Low and Edward Laight served together on a city vestry, appointed in 1777 to see to such civilian affairs as street-lighting, pump-fixing and house-renting.

By the beginning of 1779 goods of all kinds were in short supply and prices were enormously high. Firewood was in such dire demand that people tore the boards off old sheds and sawed down ornamental fruit trees illegally in the night to keep their houses warm. One man's family burned an old ship. "The ink freezes in my Pen," a diarist struggled to write. It was a harsh time in the city.

Yet for the military elite the parties and balls flourished. The Queen's birthday was celebrated in January 1780 with "uncommon Splendour and Magnificence" while in the barracks men ate biscuits that tasted like straw, and no meat. "Heaven help a Nation of Triflers," the conscience spoke again.

On the 19th of October 1781 Lord Cornwallis surrendered to General Washington at Yorktown: "Be it remembered!" joyfully wrote a New York paper from Fishkill of the surrender. With this, negotiations for peace began in Paris, and though little changed in New York for over a year, "people here in general talk much of peace."

Cold comfort the thought of peace was to men like Isaac Low, who would lose with it all they owned and believed in. They'd never wanted war, and certainly not independence; and when the goal of the contest had slid beyond economic reform they found themselves siding with their King against their neighbors. As early as 1779, when the state's rebel legislature passed an act sentencing him with other loyalists to "death without benefit of clergy," Low knew that if England lost the war he would lose all he had.

Of less prominent men like Joseph Rose and Edward Laight, who

Loyalist confidence was on the wane in the fall of 1781, but the King's son William Henry got a royal welcome when he arrived at New York just weeks before Cornwallis surrendered. Here fishermen repairing nets watch the splendidly rolling ship that bears the prince into the harbor (detail, 1781 print, Eno Collection, New York Public Library).

British and American flags flutter in turn from a Battery flagstaff — the easterly breeze seems consistent (British flag, 1731; American flag, 1793: both from the Museum of the City of New York).

had never held royal office or borne arms against the Americans, a young sailmaker's apprentice later wrote: "[They were] in a measure neutral, . . . had gathered a decent property during the contest and . . . now found it to be their true policy and interest to be silent and to keep in the background . . ." Most of them would never be troubled.

It was muddy spring in 1783 and the war was won. "The cry of peace resounds! . . . The soldiers and Hessians are moving off in bands." Though the last troops didn't leave till late November, everything was over except waiting, and people who had been gone for seven years began to return to look around. "There is no end to auctions and vendues," wrote a New Yorker back for a visit. "Everything is selling off, and I believe a great deal more than the venders can make a good title for."

At last the preparations were done. The last departing loyalist civilians were aboard ship, and the troops were rounded up to follow. "The final evacuation . . . takes place tomorrow," a man wrote to his wife, "which does not hurrie us quite so much as if the house was on fire . . ."

And on November 25, 1783, with cheering crowds on the streets, the last of the scarlet-coated British marched in cadence to their transport ship with faces determinedly as proud as on the day they'd arrived. And if they looked back to shore as their vessel stood off the Battery, they would have seen the saucy flag of the new confederacy fluttering a farewell as it whipped in the breeze.

In a boat bedecked with flags and rowed by 13 plume-hatted oarsmen, General Washington left New York to its American inhabitants on December 4, 1783. The war was over, the last of the British were gone from the harbor, and rebuilding was about to begin (Library of Congress).

Farewell . . .

"Close on the heels of an approaching winter, with an heterogenous set of inhabitants, composed of almost ruined exiles, disbanded soldiery, mixed foreigners, disaffected Tories, and the refuse of a British army, we took possession of a ruined city."

— New-York *Packet*

Gloomy as the aspect was — trees and gardens trampled and gone, houses torn up and empty, Trinity Church's topless tower ghastly — to those who came back, New York was home and heaven, the grandest place on earth. For the next five years the city turned in upon itself, absorbed in the terrific program of restoration, repair and improvement that began to prepare it for the days of glory ahead. There was little money for the job, with exports dwindled to almost nothing, and the recent source of prosperity, the soldiers, gone; but those years were loud with the clatter of carts in the street as bricks and cobblestones and lumber were trundled here and there for houses and pavements and wharfs. South Street was on the map by now, near the tip of the city, and in the upper eastern regions Front Street was planned.

The spirited optimism that the merchants threw into their rebuilding infused their ruined trade as well, and although independence closed the familiar channels of British commerce, there were new markets to win and new sources to be found for imports. On evacuation night itself, the irrepressible merchants had lifted their glasses and drunk a toast to "an uninterrupted commerce [that will] soon repair the ravages of war," and in that toast was a promise to themselves.

On a raw spring day in 1784, just months after evacuation, a little ship set sail for Canton in China, with 29 tons of ginseng stowed aboard. The *Empress of China* and her cargo were jointly owned by merchants of New York and Philadelphia, but it was from New York she sailed, and

Trinity Church was burnt in the September 1776 fire, and through the seven years of occupation its crumbling walls and tower mounted a melancholy guard over the garrison city. Green benches and lights at night made a park of the stone-strewn churchyard, to the vast disapproval of many Episcopalians, and rebuilding was delayed until 1788 (courtesy of the New-York Historical Society).

to New York she returned 15 months later with Chinese treasures — tea, silk, muslin and blue-and-white porcelain — in her hold.

A new and daring spirit of adventure had been forced on the merchants when British and American legislation closed the West Indies trade, and soon little brigs and ships with jaunty names like *Experiment* and *Enterprise* were carrying American colors up the Ganges River, into Whampoa Harbor, and to northern ports across the cold Atlantic.

Throughout the city, bringing it back to life and making it grow, were men who had been on both sides of the Revolution. After a year or so of tension, and some persecution of tories and neutrals, they sat together on new committees and societies sharing work and plans until their old differences were forgotten. The Marine Society actively encouraged the expansion of trade, while a new Society of Mechanics and Tradesmen was formed to promote American manufactures.

In Wall Street's City Hall, to be renamed Federal Hall, the United States Congress met in 1785, and the presence of the delegates brightened the city, made it gay and glad and social as it repaired its damage.

But despite ships and plans and new committees, by 1786 it was obvious that the economy of the new nation was yet unstable. Liberty had been earned but trade was needed, and defense for ships in hostile

Welcome aid for widows and children of deceased members was offered by the General Society of Mechanics and Tradesmen (left), and the building trades are represented in the vignette (above) from the 1786 membership certificate (Eno Collection, New York Public Library).

waters. America needed tariffs and laws and a government to enforce them so the states could develop and prosper. In New York, the men who had been loyal to England for those very reasons knew these things best of all.

The American Constitution was written in Philadelphia in 1787, and one by one the states began to ratify it. The following July, a few days before New York became the 11th state, a grand parade passed through cheering crowds on Broadway, dominated by the Marine Society's "federal ship" *Hamilton.* (Alexander Hamilton was a national leader in the federal movement: the Marine Society's float honored him.) Coopers, carpenters, craftsmen of all sorts marched and rode in support of union, and above them all billowed *Hamilton's* wind-filled sails as she careened down Broadway on a passage that was "not unattended by peril."

A new, stronger government was on its way in, in 1788, and it promised protected shipping for the merchants, steady employment for skillful craftsmen, and encouragement for American-made products. "The activity which reigns everywhere announces a rising prosperity," wrote French visitor Brissot de Warville, and "the music of the hammer along our wharves, the hum of busy industry" was the happy voice of a building city.

Nearly two dozen languages made a babel along the waterfront as the familiar English songs and shouts and curses mixed with French, Dutch, Spanish, Danish, Portuguese. And while New York mariners were carrying the city's commerce into foreign waters, the merchants' salesmen were wooing the trade of a broad, rich hinterland that stretched as far north as Vermont. Little by little New York came to control a back-country market once held by Boston, then by 1797 it passed Philadelphia in the volume of its export trade, and it was still growing.

Now, 62 years old in 1797, Joseph Rose knew the joy of living in a city that prospered in time of peace. He'd come through the war with his

The British withdrew from a city whose streets and shores looked like this. The built-up town extended little beyond Joseph Rose's Water Street house on the east side, but streets were already laid out for a suburban neighborhood around the Bowery Lane. Wealthy landholders' formal gardens show as dark squares with formal crosses indicating their beds and walks (courtesy of the New-York Historical Society).

New York's old City Hall, transformed by French architect Pierre L'Enfant, stands brilliant and beautiful as the nation's Federal Hall. In it the United States Congress met in 1785, on its iron-railed balcony Washington took office as first American president, as shown here, on April 30, 1789 (Museum of the City of New York).

modest fortune intact, and when prices were low in 1791 he'd moved his family into a little house at the "court end" of Pearl Street within sight of the Battery. With Edward Laight he'd built a new dock behind the houses on the Water Street wharf for bigger ships; and he'd opened a distillery of his own on Ferry Street. There was time, in these later years, for private pleasures: a pipe of good tobacco from his store, a bottle of wine brought in on *Industry* 20 years before, evenings with the Calliopean Society passed in pleasant debate on theoretical questions. (Is Man happier in the married state, or single? the husband of 31 years pondered. Should women be suffered to vote?)

Confident in the city's northward growth, Rose joined thousands of New Yorkers in real estate speculation in 1791, buying land in a grassy Out Ward meadow beside streets marked only by stakes and string. And four sons and three daughters were growing up well. Elizabeth, Mary and Ann all married businessmen; Joseph, jr. joined his father as a merchant and distiller; Samuel trained as a mariner, then went awhile to Charleston where Roses had long been in commerce; Isaac apprenticed to a druggist and became an apothecary; and William may have made his father proudest of all when he became an attorney and one of the Masters in the Court of Chancery. William would later found and edit the New York *Morning Post,* using it to support the Republican party in which he became earnestly involved.

All in all, as the 18th century came to its end, Joseph Rose could have

This tall-porticoed house at the bottom of Bowling Green (above), New York's grandest but not its most beautiful residence, was built in 1790. It was meant to be the president's mansion, but Congress left New York before Washington could live in it. It is shown here in 1797 when it was governor John Jay's house. Cows resting comfortably in its horseshoe drive have little respect for its grandeur, and a passing cartman gives it not a glance. Houses shown in the detail below are built like Joseph Rose's, with brick fronts and clapboard side walls (courtesy of the New-York Historical Society).

looked back on a life that had been good and rich and peaceful although it had perforce been lived in a period of immense stress and changing order. He had never been famous, never distinguished himself particularly, but he had reason to be proud of the things he'd managed to do.

Isaac Sears, Rose could have reflected, hadn't been so fortunate. Harrassed by creditors just three years after the peace, he'd gone out on board the trading ship *Hope* to Canton hoping to improve his business. He'd fallen ill instead, died in Whampoa Harbor, and was buried on faraway French Island. Nor had Isaac Low fared well. He'd gone to England after the evacuation, but his loyalty had been questioned by the Crown. Humiliated and in poverty, he had died in 1791.

The 18th century was closing, and with it passed the first bright days of the new republic. There was to be more trouble before there was peace again, but New York was moving quickly now toward its most brilliant decades — the Age of Sail — that began in earnest in 1815.

But in 1790 Congress left New York — though its going deprived the city of little but superficial excitement — and by 1800 there were tremors of a new commercial crisis. American vessels in the Atlantic and Caribbean waters they knew so well were falling prey to French and English privateers, and along the hostile shores of North Africa the

Distilleries like this one made rum from the thick brown molasses of the West Indies. A good fire made vapor rise from the bubbling liquid in the brick-walled vats, and the vapor condensed to pure rum as it spiralled through copper tubing to the firkins on the floor. Joseph Rose, who had been in the West Indies trade, became a distiller in 1786.

Tripolitan pirates were getting bolder and more demanding as they forced tribute money from American captains.

Hoping to deprive England and France of the supplies they needed to continue hostilities with each other, president Thomas Jefferson declared an embargo in December 1807, cutting off exports from all American ports. Incredibly unpopular in seaport towns, the embargo did more harm to American merchants than it did to warring Europeans. And it encouraged American smuggling that supplied both hostile forces with goods and let them laugh at the embargo!

An English visitor, John Lambert, described the New York waterfront just before the embargo became effective. The port was "filled with shipping and the wharfs were crowded with commodities of

A barefooted boy and a baby stroll down a rutted lane (Clinton Street) toward the clustered gambrel- and gable-roofed houses on the northern harbor streets. Though cows and horses still graze in grassy pastures and big wooden farmhouses stand on the hills to the right, the city's northward growth is apparent when this 1794 view is compared to the one taken 31 years earlier on page 10 (Museum of the City of New York).

One of the liveliest views of the 18th century city, Francis Guy's painting was made around 1797. Though its subject is the Tontine Coffee House (left), its substance is the busy working life of a seaport street. Men on the Tontine porch stand talking, while just below, a clutter of barrels and crates, goods and men barricade Wall Street near its intersection with Water. From the wood building across the street the wares of a furniture seller spill temptingly onto the sidewalk, and down toward the wharf an auctioneer (near right) holds court from a packing-crate platform (courtesy of the New-York Historical Society).

every description . . . All was noise and bustle. . . . . carters driving in
every direction . . . sailors and labourers on the wharfs . . . the merchants and clerks . . . in their counting-houses or upon the piers . . ."

But five months later the place looked as if it were dead. "[It was]
indeed full of shipping; but they were dismantled and laid up . . .
scarcely a sailor to be found . . . counting-houses shut up . . . the grass
had begun to grow upon the wharfs."

America was going to war again with England: the War of 1812 was
fought for "Free Trade and Sailors' Rights," but though commerce
would lie nearly dormant for seven more years, spirits were high and
the city was growing.

In 1807 South Street was nearly complete all the way up to the shipyards, and John Lambert had noticed that the warehouses lining it were "nearly all new buildings." New York was supreme among American commercial cities as the war came on, and even as their ships rocked quietly at the wharfs the merchants went on buying waterfront land and putting up warehouses on it. Even as Castle Clinton was being finished near the Battery for the city's defense in 1811, shipchandler Peter Schermerhorn was beginning the full blockfront of warehouses on Beekman Slip that have come to us today as Schermerhorn Row.

New York soared brilliantly toward commercial greatness then, slowed only briefly by that second war with England. And in this astounding success, she fulfilled the promise inherent in the generation of merchants who lived through the revolutionary years. Reasonable wisdom, respect for the daily exactions of trade, opposition to things that hurt commerce. Those considerations had guided them to protest the Sugar Act and the Stamp Act, guided some of them to stay neutral in New York during the Revolution, guided them to support the Constitution, guided them to move toward 1815 with confidence in the future of their business and their city.

When 1815 came, most of the men who'd been adults in the colonial and federal city were gone or retired. Joseph Rose died at 72, ten months before the embargo in 1807. But let this be recalled: the lives of these very men laid down the foundations on which New York's 19th century magnificence in trade was built.

This looks like a summer scene, as merchants seem to work with frantic haste laying in goods for selling-season in the fall (detail, Tontine Coffee House, courtesy of the New-York Historical Society).

Note on Captain Joseph Rose and His House

Since for the sake of space and readability footnotes have not been used in *Farewell to Old England,* this end note on the man and his life will point out the places where conjecture has necessarily replaced documented fact in the text's presentation of him.

We know for sure only three things about Captain Rose before 1770. He was born in 1735 (he died at the age of 72 in 1807); he married Barbary Egburson, whose descendants spell her name Barbara Egbertson, in 1766 (their New York marriage bond is recorded in Liber X page 68); and he was one of the founders of New York's Marine Society in 1769.

It is safe to guess that Joseph Rose was trained as a mariner (it was as "mariner" that he bought his first real estate in 1771); and it is further likely that he spent some of his time aboard the coastal and West Indies trading sloop *Industry,* shown in newspaper customs-house reports as commanded by one James Rose. (Joseph Rose later named his own brig *Industry,* and he plied the same Atlantic and Caribbean trade.) In September 1770, Joseph Rose entered the shipping news columns as "Captain Rose."

Our documentary knowledge of Rose begins in October 1771, when he bought his first real estate, the easterly half of a double lot on Water Street between Peck Slip and Dover Street from the executors of Gerrit Van Horne. Two surveys, one made late in the 18th century by Evert or Gerard Bancker, and one made in 1804 by Joseph F. Mangin, establish Rose's property as the lot where No. 273 Water Street stands today. From this point on, Rose's career clears up, because he delighted in running advertisements in the New York papers. On March 15, 1773, "Captain Joseph Rose" advertised in the *Mercury* rooms to let in the house "which [he] now lives in."

We are not certain that the house that Rose advertised in 1773 is the same house that stands (much altered) at 273 Water Street today. A house very much like it, belonging to Edward Laight, stood next door and was described in a survey of 1778 or 1779. Evidence recently located by Regina Kellerman suggests that Laight rebuilt his house in 1780, and since the Rose and Laight houses are known to have shared a cartway to the wharf (first mentioned when Common Council scheduled its repaving in 1797), Rose might have rebuilt as well. But in May 1786, Rose advertised his "three story house" at 135 Water Street (it became No. 273 by 1794), and the likelihood is that that house remains, worn and empty, on Water Street today.

The little building has not survived without change. It was burned and rebuilt in 1904, and today only the foundations, the second story front and a little of the ground floor front remain as built. But they are a powerful link with this city's past and with a merchant mariner, typical of thousands of others, who lived through the Revolution. Rose's house is important historically rather than architecturally, and it should be preserved and interpreted as a primary link with the 18th century city. These links are rare and precious for us in New York today.

South Street's Books

The South Street Seaport Museum has published a series of small books that explore the 18th and 19th century roots of New York as a seaport city. All of the books can be ordered by mail from the museum's Publications Department, 203 Front Street, New York, N. Y. 10038. Please add $.50 per title for packaging and handling, and New York residents please add 8% sales tax. A full catalogue with these and other titles is available for $.25.

Seaport City: New York 1775, by Floyd M. Shumway. 64 pages, illustrations, maps, bibliography. $1.95.

It was exciting to be in New York on the eve of the Revolution. The urban center of one of the central colonies, it was involved in all of the prewar agitation over British policy, it knew all the malaise of the situation which had already become acknowledged conflict. Dr. Shumway's book is a window on the city and its people in the troubled times from which New York emerged ready to grow into America's greatest port city.

Counting-house Days in South Street; New York's early brick seaport buildings, by Ellen F. Rosebrock. 48 pages, illustrations, map. $2.50

The old brick buildings at South Street are the warehouses, and within them the counting-houses, where the grand old merchants of New York's age of sail laid their plans and stored their goods. This book is an architectural history of the 19th century warehouses. It also tells the story of merchants and their clerks and the way their days passed in their seaport buildings.

Ships & the River, a Coloring Book Guide to South Street, by David Canright. 32 pages to color and read. $2.00

All of South Street's ships, shown at their old jobs or at home at their docks, are here to color; and there are pictures of people at work aboard them or restoring them. Lively captions introduce young readers to the harbor life they can see from South Street's busy piers.

South Street around 1900, by Peter Stanford. 33 pages, illustrations. $1.50

Here are the photographs taken along the East River waterfront during the last years when the city looked like "old New York." Here, in Thomas Kennedy's pictures, are the square-rigged ships and their crews; here, too, are early lunch-time river-watchers, the Wall Street brokers who came to the docks to relax then as they do today. A few of Kennedy's New England pictures, scenes in small wood-built fishing towns, are included as well.

A Fisherman's Breeze; the Log of the Ruth M. Martin, by A. Graham Miles. 102 pages, illustrations. $2.50

In 1904 young stockbroker Graham Miles celebrated his twenty-ninth birthday with an adventure he'd dreamed about through countless summer lunchtimes spent on the docks near the Fulton Fish Market. That September he shipped out on a two-week voyage on the Gloucesterman *Ruth M. Martin,* a fishing schooner much like South Street's graceful *Lettie G. Howard.* Through sun and squall, Miles kept his journal, recording in gentle language life in the immemorial pattern of the fisherman.